MW01635807

This is Chris Moose.

Hello!

It’s Chris Moose time!

Look, a Chris Moose tree!

Rockin' around
the Chris Moose tree.

Chris Moose, the snow's
coming down!

I'm watching
it fall.

It's a Chris Moose party.

Yes, I'm going to a party.

Welcome
Chris Moose,
come this
way.

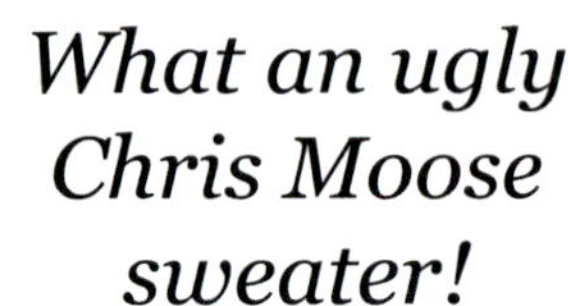

Ha ha!

That's a blue, blue Chris Moose.

This is Carole.

Hello!

Who's that?
I like his sweater...

That's Chris Moose, Carole.

Let it snow!

Marry Chris Moose?

Yes, this Chris Moose
will be a very special
Chris Moose to me!

That's a holly jolly
Chris Moose!

It's the moose wonderful time of the year!

Father Chris Moose.

It’s beginning to look a lot like
Chris Moose.

Merry Chris Moose baby.

There is nothing better
than being with family

for Chris Moose.

Chris Moose cards

Chris Moose
VISA REWARDS
1.866.661.3377
010

Meadow Hockey Association
Chris Moose

Christopher A Moose
123 Forest Path
Meadow BC
Canada
DRIVER'S LICENCE

This story was written by **Andrew Bond**. During the day, as a classroom teacher, he reads books to kids to try to keep them awake. In the evening, as a father of three, he reads books to his kids to try to put them to sleep. Sometimes he writes books for kids. Other times he runs his business, West Coast Forest School (look it up). Occasionally he sleeps. He lives with his beautiful wife and family in Victoria, B.C. It is a nice place. You should visit.

Melanie Bond has a Master's Degree in Fine Arts from UBC. She loves photography, drawing and painting in the great outdoors-surrounded by nature, wind and weather. Her art has been exhibited worldwide and is in many collections across Canada.
One day she saw Chris Moose hiding behind a rhododendron at Van Dusen Gardens and she just had to draw him. True story. She loves living in Vancouver, B.C. She occasionally visits her son Andrew and his family in Victoria.

Book and cover design by: Melanie Bond and Halima Qureshi

ISBN: 978-1-9990675-0-2

Published by West Coast Forest School.
Saanich, BC, Canada
westcoastforestschool.ca

Printed and bound by First Choice Books & Victoria Bindery
Victoria, BC, Canada